Simple & Delicious

CURRIES

Simple & Delicious
CURRIES

OVER 100 SENSATIONAL RECIPES FOR CURRY LOVERS

This edition published in 2012
LOVE FOOD is an imprint of Parragon Books Ltd

Parragon
Queen Street House
4 Queen Street
Bath BA1 1HE, UK

ISBN: 978-1-4454-8266-8

Printed in China

Cover Design by Geoff Borin
Additional Photography by Bob Wheeler
Additional Food Styling by Sandra Baddeley
Introduction by Anne Sheasby

Notes for the Reader
This book uses both metric and imperial measurements. Follow the same units of measurement throughout; do not mix metric and imperial. All spoon measurements are level: teaspoons are assumed to be 5 ml, and tablespoons are assumed to be 15 ml. Unless otherwise stated, milk is assumed to be full fat, eggs and individual vegetables are medium, and pepper is freshly ground black pepper. Unless otherwise stated, all root vegetables should be washed and peeled prior to using.

Garnishes, decorations and serving suggestions are all optional and not necessarily included in the recipe ingredients or method.

The times given are an approximate guide only. Preparation times differ according to the techniques used by different people and the cooking times may also vary from those given. Optional ingredients, variations or serving suggestions have not been included in the time calculations.

Recipes using raw or very lightly cooked eggs should be avoided by infants, the elderly, pregnant women, convalescents and anyone suffering from an illness. Pregnant and breastfeeding women are advised to avoid eating peanuts and peanut products. Sufferers from nut allergies should be aware that some of the ready-made ingredients used in the recipes in this book may contain nuts. Always check the packaging before use.

Vegetarians should be aware that some of the ready-made ingredients used in the recipes in this book may contain animal products. Always check the packaging before use.

Contents

Introduction

Curries are associated with many Asian countries, such as India, Bangladesh, Pakistan, Sri Lanka, Thailand, Indonesia and Malaysia. Some other regions around the globe, such as South Africa, the Caribbean, Singapore and Vietnam, also have their own versions of curry-based dishes.

Over the centuries, curries have become a popular choice in many countries worldwide. Today there are many great establishments producing and serving excellent curry dishes, but, as this cookbook demonstrates, curries are quick and easy to make at home. By combining a selection of fresh ingredients and spices, you will soon be creating tempting curries in your own kitchen.

Origins of Curry

It is believed that the term *curry* originates from the Tamil word *kari* which means 'spiced sauce'. Originally the word curry referred to a combination of ingredients stewed together with liquid and various spices to create a sauce or type of casserole. These days, partly due to its migration to many regions of the world, curry has now taken on a wider meaning. Generally speaking, the term curry now denotes a variety of dishes comprising a combination of ingredients cooked together to create a range of savoury, often sauce-based, dishes all of which are spiced.

Curries vary from one region to another – some are creamy and mild, such as Korma, others, such as Madras, tend to be medium-hot, while curries like Vindaloo are the really hot and spicy ones.

To complete the meal, curries are often served with a range of appetising accompaniments including naan bread, chapatis, pilau rice, mango chutney, lime pickle, raita and so on. Again, the selection of accompaniments will vary according to the choice of the main dish.

Spices

A combination of spices, usually in the form of ground spices or a spice paste, is an essential component of a curry. Ready-made powders and pastes are widely available, but it is preferable to buy whole, dried spices and grind or crush them yourself at home, as required.

A clean electric coffee grinder (kept specifically for spices) is an ideal way to grind your own spices. Alternatively, a pestle and mortar can be used. You will find that grinding or crushing your own spices will bring out their lovely aromatic flavours and will vastly improve the taste of your dishes. Try dry-frying whole spices in a heavy-based frying pan over a moderate heat for a few minutes before grinding them – this will help to bring out their flavour even more.

The blend of spices used to make a basic curry powder or paste varies enormously from region to region, but spices commonly used in curry-making include coriander, cumin, fenugreek and mustard seeds, black peppercorns, turmeric, chillies, cardamom, cinnamon, cloves and sometimes ground ginger. It very much depends on personal taste and how hot you like your curry to be, so choose a mixture of spices that suits your palate best.

Storing Spices

It is best to buy whole spices in small quantities to ensure that they remain as fresh as possible. Once freshly ground to a fine powder, spice mixtures should keep well in an airtight container for up to a month. However, ground spices do deteriorate quite quickly so, if possible, it is best to grind spices fresh each time you cook.

If you do buy ready-ground spices, make sure that you store them in a cool, dark, dry place and preferably not in glass jars in a spice rack on the kitchen wall – this may look attractive but it is probably the worst way to store dried spices.

Other Ingredients

Other ingredients, such as onions, tomatoes, garlic, fresh ginger, coconut, tamarind and fresh coriander, play an important role in many curries. Chillies, both fresh and dried,

are also an essential ingredient in numerous curry dishes.

The majority of chillies are green when they are unripe (or immature) and they then ripen to varying shades of red. The colour of a fresh chilli is not an indication of how hot the flavour of the chilli will be. As a general rule, the smaller and thinner the chilli, the hotter it will be. You can reduce the heat of a fresh chilli by cutting the chilli in half lengthways and scraping out the seeds and core (or membranes) before use.

When preparing fresh chillies, it is a good idea to wear disposable gloves, as the natural oils in chillies may cause irritation to your skin and eyes. If you don't have any gloves, make sure you wash your hands thoroughly after preparing chillies.

Thai Red Curry Paste

1 tbsp coriander seeds

1 tbsp cumin seeds

2 tsp shrimp paste

12 dried or fresh red chillies, chopped

2 shallots, chopped

8 garlic cloves, chopped

2.5-cm/1-inch piece fresh galangal, chopped

2 lemon grass stalks (white part only), chopped

4 kaffir lime leaves, chopped

2 tbsp chopped fresh coriander root

grated rind of 1 lime

1 tsp black peppercorns

Dry fry the coriander and cumin seeds in a frying pan, stirring constantly, for 2–3 minutes until browned. Remove from the heat and grind to a powder using a pestle and mortar. Wrap the shrimp paste in a piece of aluminium foil and grill or dry fry in a frying pan for 2–3 minutes, turning once or twice. Put the ground spices, shrimp paste and chillies in a food processor or blender and process until finely chopped. Add the remaining ingredients and process again to a smooth paste, scraping down the sides as necessary.

Thai Green Curry Paste

Follow the instructions for Thai Red Curry Paste, but replace the chillies with 15 fresh green Thai chillies, use only 6 garlic cloves, increase the number of kaffir lime leaves to 6, and add 1 teaspoon of salt with the pepper.

Thai Yellow Curry Paste

3 small fresh orange or yellow chillies, coarsely chopped

3 large garlic cloves, coarsely chopped

4 shallots, coarsely chopped

3 tsp ground turmeric

1 tsp salt

12–15 black peppercorns

1 lemon grass stalk (white part only), coarsely chopped

2.5-cm/1-inch piece fresh root ginger, chopped

Put all the ingredients in a food processor or blender and process to a thick paste, scraping down the sides as necessary.

Mussaman Curry Paste

4 large dried red chillies, stalks removed

2 tsp shrimp paste

3 shallots, finely chopped

3 garlic cloves, finely chopped

2.5-cm/1-inch piece fresh galangal, finely
    chopped

2 lemon grass stalks (white part only), finely
    chopped

2 cloves

1 tbsp coriander seeds

1 tbsp cumin seeds

seeds from 3 green cardamom pods

1 tsp black peppercorns

1 tsp salt

Place the chillies in a bowl, cover with hot
water and set aside to soak for 30–45 minutes.
Wrap the shrimp paste in aluminium foil and
grill or dry fry in a frying pan for 2–3 minutes,
turning once or twice. Remove from the grill
or frying pan. Dry fry the shallots, garlic,
galangal, lemon grass, cloves, and coriander,
cumin and cardamom seeds over a low heat,
stirring frequently, for 3–4 minutes until lightly
browned. Transfer to a food processor and
process until finely ground. Add the chillies
and their soaking liquid, peppercorns and salt
and process again. Add the shrimp paste and
process again to a smooth paste, scraping
down the sides as necessary.

Garlic & Ginger Paste

Blend together equal quantities of garlic and
fresh root ginger. Store in a sealed jar in the
refrigerator for up to 3 weeks, or in a freezer
for up to 1 month.

Poultry & Meat

Chicken Tikka Masala

serves 4–6

400 g/14 oz canned chopped tomatoes

300 ml/10 fl oz double cream

1 cooked tandoori chicken, cut into 8 pieces

salt and pepper

fresh chopped coriander, to garnish

cooked basmati rice, to serve

tikka masala

25 g/1 oz ghee or 2 tbsp vegetable oil or groundnut oil

1 large garlic clove, finely chopped

1 fresh red chilli, deseeded and chopped

2 tsp ground cumin

2 tsp ground paprika

½ tsp salt

pepper

To make the tikka masala, heat a large frying pan with a lid over a medium heat, then add the ghee. Add the garlic and chilli and stir-fry for 1 minute. Stir in the cumin, paprika, and salt and pepper to taste and continue stirring for about 30 seconds.

Stir the tomatoes and cream into the pan. Reduce the heat to low and leave to simmer for about 10 minutes, stirring frequently, until it reduces and thickens.

Meanwhile, remove all the bones and skin from the chicken pieces, then cut the meat into bite-sized pieces.

Adjust the seasoning of the sauce, if necessary. Add the chicken pieces to the pan, cover and leave to simmer for 3–5 minutes until the chicken is heated through. Garnish with coriander and serve immediately with rice.

Chicken Korma

serves 4

1 chicken, weighing
1.3 kg/3 lb

225 g/8 oz ghee or butter

3 onions, thinly sliced

1 garlic clove, crushed

2.5-cm/1-inch piece fresh
root ginger, grated

1 tsp mild chilli powder

1 tsp ground turmeric

1 tsp ground coriander

½ tsp ground cardamom

½ tsp ground cinnamon

½ tsp salt

1 tbsp gram flour

125 ml/4 fl oz milk

500 ml/18 fl oz double
cream

fresh coriander leaves,
to garnish

freshly cooked rice,
to serve

Put the chicken into a large saucepan, cover with water and bring to the boil. Reduce the heat, cover and simmer for 30 minutes. Remove from the heat, lift out the chicken and set aside to cool. Reserve 125 ml/4 fl oz of the cooking liquid. Remove and discard the skin and bones. Cut the flesh into bite-sized pieces.

Heat the ghee in a large saucepan over a medium heat. Add the onions and garlic and cook, stirring, for 3 minutes, or until softened. Add the ginger, chilli powder, turmeric, ground coriander, cardamom, cinnamon and salt and cook for a further 5 minutes. Add the chicken and the reserved cooking liquid. Cook for 2 minutes.

Blend the flour with a little of the milk and add to the pan, then stir in the remaining milk. Bring to the boil, stirring, then reduce the heat, cover and simmer for 25 minutes. Stir in the cream, cover and simmer for a further 15 minutes.

Garnish with coriander leaves and serve with freshly cooked rice.

Chicken Jalfrezi

serves 4

½ tsp cumin seeds

½ tsp coriander seeds

1 tsp mustard oil

3 tbsp vegetable oil

1 large onion, finely chopped

3 garlic cloves, crushed

1 tbsp tomato purée

2 tomatoes, peeled and chopped

1 tsp ground turmeric

½ tsp chilli powder

½ tsp garam masala

1 tsp red wine vinegar

1 small red pepper, deseeded and chopped

125 g/4½ oz frozen broad beans

500 g/1 lb 2 oz cooked chicken, chopped

salt

sprigs of fresh coriander, to garnish

freshly cooked rice, to serve

Grind the cumin and coriander seeds in a mortar with a pestle, then reserve. Heat the mustard oil in a large, heavy-based frying pan over a high heat for 1 minute, or until it begins to smoke. Add the vegetable oil, reduce the heat and add the onion and garlic. Cook for 10 minutes, or until golden.

Add the tomato purée, tomatoes, turmeric, chilli powder, garam masala, vinegar and reserved ground cumin and coriander seeds to the frying pan. Stir the mixture until fragrant.

Add the red pepper and broad beans and stir for a further 2 minutes, or until the pepper is softened. Stir in the chicken, and season to taste with salt. Simmer gently for 6–8 minutes, or until the chicken is heated through and the beans are tender. Transfer to warmed serving bowls, garnish with sprigs of coriander and serve with freshly cooked rice.

Thai Green Chicken Curry

serves 4

2 tbsp groundnut or sunflower oil

2 tbsp Thai green curry paste

500 g/1 lb 2 oz skinless, boneless chicken breasts, cut into cubes

2 kaffir lime leaves, roughly torn

1 lemon grass stalk, finely chopped

225 ml/8 fl oz coconut milk

16 baby aubergines, halved

2 tbsp Thai fish sauce

sprigs of fresh Thai basil and thinly sliced kaffir lime leaves, to garnish

Heat the oil in a preheated wok or large, heavy-based frying pan. Add the curry paste and stir-fry briefly until all the aromas are released.

Add the chicken, lime leaves and lemon grass and stir-fry for 3–4 minutes, until the meat is beginning to colour. Add the coconut milk and aubergines and simmer gently for 8–10 minutes, or until tender.

Stir in the fish sauce and serve immediately, garnished with sprigs of Thai basil and lime leaves.

Balti Chicken

serves 6

3 tbsp ghee or vegetable oil

2 large onions, sliced

3 tomatoes, sliced

½ tsp kalonji seeds

4 black peppercorns

2 cardamom pods

1 cinnamon stick

1 tsp chilli powder

1 tsp garam masala

2 tsp garlic and ginger paste

700 g/1 lb 9 oz skinless, boneless chicken breasts or thighs, diced

2 tbsp natural yogurt

2 tbsp chopped fresh coriander, plus extra sprigs to garnish

2 fresh green chillies, deseeded and finely chopped

2 tbsp lime juice

salt

Heat the ghee in a large, heavy-based frying pan. Add the onions and cook over a low heat, stirring occasionally, for 10 minutes, or until golden. Add the tomatoes, kalonji seeds, peppercorns, cardamom pods, cinnamon stick, chilli powder, garam masala, and garlic and ginger paste, and season to taste with salt. Cook, stirring constantly, for 5 minutes.

Add the chicken and cook, stirring constantly, for 5 minutes, or until well coated in the spice paste. Stir in the yogurt. Cover and simmer, stirring occasionally, for 10 minutes.

Stir in the chopped coriander, chillies and lime juice. Transfer to a warmed serving dish, garnish with sprigs of coriander and serve immediately.

Lamb Rogan Josh

serves 4

350 ml/12 fl oz natural yogurt

½ tsp ground asafoetida dissolved in 2 tbsp water

700 g/1 lb 9 oz boneless leg of lamb, trimmed and cut into 5-cm/2-inch cubes

2 tomatoes, deseeded and chopped

1 onion, chopped

25 g/1 oz ghee or 2 tbsp vegetable or groundnut oil

1½ tbsp garlic and ginger paste

2 tbsp tomato purée

2 bay leaves

1 tbsp ground coriander

¼–1 tsp chilli powder, ideally Kashmiri chilli powder

½ tsp ground turmeric

1 tsp salt

½ tsp garam masala

Put the yogurt in a large bowl and stir in the dissolved asafoetida. Add the lamb and use your hands to rub in all the marinade, then set aside for 30 minutes.

Meanwhile, put the tomatoes and onion in a blender and process until blended.

Heat the ghee in a flameproof casserole or large frying pan with a tight-fitting lid. Add the garlic and ginger paste and stir around until the aromas are released. Stir in the tomato mixture, tomato purée, bay leaves, coriander, chilli powder and turmeric, reduce the heat to low and simmer, stirring occasionally, for 5–8 minutes.

Add the lamb and salt with any leftover marinade and stir around for 2 minutes. Cover, reduce the heat to low and simmer, stirring occasionally, for 30 minutes. The lamb should give off enough moisture to prevent it catching on the base of the pan, but if the sauce looks too dry, stir in a little water.

Sprinkle the lamb with the garam masala, re-cover the pan and continue simmering for 15–20 minutes until the lamb is tender. Serve immediately.

Lamb, Tomato & Aubergine Curry

serves 4

2 tbsp oil

500 g/1 lb 2 oz lamb fillet or leg, cut into cubes

1 large onion, coarsely chopped

2–3 tbsp curry paste

1 aubergine, cut into small cubes

10 tomatoes, peeled, deseeded and coarsely chopped

400 ml/14 fl oz coconut milk

300 ml/10 fl oz lamb stock

2 tbsp chopped fresh coriander, plus extra sprigs to garnish

Heat the oil in a large frying pan. Add the lamb in batches and cook for 8–10 minutes, or until browned all over. Remove with a slotted spoon and reserve.

Add the onion to the frying pan and cook for 2–3 minutes, or until just softened. Add the curry paste and stir-fry for a further 2 minutes. Add the aubergine, three-quarters of the tomatoes and the lamb and stir together.

Add the coconut milk and stock and simmer gently for 30–40 minutes, until the lamb is tender and the curry has thickened.

Mix the remaining tomatoes and the chopped coriander together in a small bowl, then stir into the curry. Garnish with sprigs of coriander and serve immediately.

Lamb Do Piaza

serves 4

4 onions, sliced into rings

3 garlic cloves, coarsely chopped

2.5-cm/1-inch piece fresh root ginger, grated

1 tsp ground coriander

1 tsp ground cumin

1 tsp chilli powder

½ tsp ground turmeric

1 tsp ground cinnamon

1 tsp garam masala

4 tbsp water

5 tbsp ghee or vegetable oil

600 g/1 lb 5 oz boneless lamb, cut into bite-sized chunks

6 tbsp natural yogurt

salt and pepper

fresh coriander leaves, to garnish

freshly cooked rice, to serve

Put half of the onions into a food processor with the garlic, ginger, ground coriander, cumin, chilli powder, turmeric, cinnamon and garam masala. Add the water and process to a paste.

Heat 4 tablespoons of the ghee in a saucepan over a medium heat. Add the remaining onions and cook, stirring, for 3 minutes. Remove from the heat. Lift out the onions with a slotted spoon and set aside. Heat the remaining ghee in the pan over a high heat, add the lamb and cook, stirring, for 5 minutes. Lift out the meat and drain on kitchen paper.

Add the onion paste to the pan and cook over a medium heat, stirring, until the oil separates. Stir in the yogurt, season to taste with salt and pepper, return the lamb to the pan and stir well.

Bring the mixture gently to the boil, reduce the heat, cover and simmer for 25 minutes. Stir in the reserved onion rings and cook for a further 5 minutes. Remove from the heat, and garnish with coriander leaves. Serve immediately with freshly cooked rice.

Lamb Pasanda

serves 4–6

600 g/1 lb 5 oz boneless shoulder or leg of lamb

2 tbsp garlic and ginger paste

55 g/2 oz ghee or 4 tbsp vegetable or groundnut oil

3 large onions, chopped

1 fresh green chilli, deseeded and chopped

2 green cardamom pods, lightly crushed

1 cinnamon stick, broken in half

2 tsp ground coriander

1 tsp ground cumin

1 tsp ground turmeric

250 ml/9 fl oz water

150 ml/5 fl oz double cream

4 tbsp ground almonds

1½ tsp salt

1 tsp garam masala

paprika and toasted flaked almonds, to garnish

freshly cooked rice, to serve

Cut the meat into thin slices, then place the slices between clingfilm and pound with a rolling pin or meat mallet to make them even thinner. Put the lamb slices in a bowl, add the garlic and ginger paste and use your hands to rub the paste into the lamb. Cover and set aside in a cool place to marinate for 2 hours.

Heat the ghee in a large frying pan with a tight-fitting lid over a medium-high heat. Add the onions and chilli and cook, stirring frequently, for 5–8 minutes until the onions are golden brown.

Stir in the cardamom pods, cinnamon stick, coriander, cumin and turmeric and continue stirring for 2 minutes, or until the spices are aromatic.

Add the meat to the pan and cook, stirring occasionally, for about 5 minutes until it is brown on all sides and the fat begins to separate. Stir in the water and bring to the boil, still stirring. Reduce the heat to its lowest setting, cover the pan tightly and simmer for 40 minutes, or until the meat is tender.

When the lamb is tender, stir the cream and ground almonds together in a bowl. Beat in 6 tablespoons of the hot cooking liquid from the pan, then gradually beat this mixture back into the pan. Stir in the salt and garam masala. Continue to simmer for a further 5 minutes, uncovered, stirring occasionally.

Garnish with a sprinkling of paprika and toasted flaked almonds and serve with freshly cooked rice.

Lamb & Spinach Curry

serves 2–4

300 ml/10 fl oz vegetable oil

2 onions, sliced

¼ bunch of fresh coriander

2 fresh green chillies, chopped

1½ tsp finely chopped fresh root ginger

1½ tsp crushed fresh garlic

1 tsp chilli powder

½ tsp ground turmeric

450 g/1 lb lean lamb, cut into bite-sized chunks

1 tsp salt

1 kg/2 lb 4 oz fresh spinach, trimmed, washed and chopped

700 ml/1¼ pints water

finely chopped fresh red chilli, to garnish

Heat the oil in a large, heavy-based frying pan. Add the onions and cook until light golden.

Add the fresh coriander and green chillies to the frying pan and stir-fry for 3–5 minutes. Reduce the heat and add the ginger, garlic, chilli powder and turmeric, stirring well.

Add the lamb to the frying pan and stir-fry for a further 5 minutes. Add the salt and the spinach and cook, stirring occasionally with a wooden spoon, for a further 3–5 minutes.

Add the water, stirring, and cook over a low heat, covered, for 45 minutes. Remove the lid and check the meat. If it is not tender, turn the meat over, increase the heat and cook, uncovered, until the surplus water has been absorbed. Stir-fry the mixture for a further 5–7 minutes.

Transfer the lamb and spinach mixture to a serving dish and garnish with chopped red chilli. Serve hot.

Pork with Cinnamon & Fenugreek

serves 4

1 tsp ground coriander

1 tsp ground cumin

1 tsp chilli powder

1 tbsp dried fenugreek leaves (methi)

1 tsp ground fenugreek

150 ml/5 fl oz natural yogurt

450 g/1 lb diced pork fillet

4 tbsp ghee or vegetable oil

1 large onion, sliced

5-cm/2-inch piece fresh root ginger, finely chopped

4 garlic cloves, finely chopped

1 cinnamon stick

6 cardamom pods

6 whole cloves

2 bay leaves

175 ml/6 fl oz water

salt

Mix the coriander, cumin, chilli powder, dried fenugreek, ground fenugreek and yogurt together in a small bowl. Place the pork in a large, shallow, non-metallic dish and add the spice mixture, turning well to coat. Cover with clingfilm and leave to marinate in the refrigerator for 30 minutes.

Heat the ghee in a large, heavy-based saucepan. Cook the onion over a low heat, stirring occasionally, for 5 minutes, or until softened. Add the ginger, garlic, cinnamon stick, cardamom pods, cloves and bay leaves and cook, stirring constantly, for 2 minutes, or until the spices give off their aroma. Add the meat with its marinade and the water, and season to taste with salt. Bring to the boil, reduce the heat, cover and simmer for 30 minutes.

Transfer the meat mixture to a preheated wok or large, heavy-based frying pan and cook over a low heat, stirring constantly, until dry and tender. If necessary, occasionally sprinkle with a little water to prevent it sticking to the wok. Serve immediately.

Red Curry Pork with Peppers

serves 4

2 tbsp vegetable or groundnut oil

1 onion, coarsely chopped

2 garlic cloves, chopped

450 g/1 lb pork fillet, thickly sliced

1 red pepper, deseeded and cut into squares

175 g/6 oz mushrooms, quartered

2 tbsp Thai red curry paste

115 g/4 oz creamed coconut, chopped

300 ml/10 fl oz pork or vegetable stock

2 tbsp Thai soy sauce

4 tomatoes, peeled, deseeded and chopped

handful of fresh coriander, chopped

Heat the oil in a wok or large frying pan and cook the onion and garlic for 1–2 minutes, until they are softened but not browned.

Add the pork slices and stir-fry for 2–3 minutes until browned all over. Add the pepper, mushrooms and curry paste.

Dissolve the coconut in the stock and add to the wok with the soy sauce. Bring to the boil and simmer for 4–5 minutes until the liquid has reduced and thickened.

Add the tomatoes and coriander and cook for 1–2 minutes before serving.

Pork Vindaloo

serves 4–6

4 tbsp mustard oil

2 large onions, finely chopped

6 bay leaves

6 cloves

6 garlic cloves, chopped

3 green cardamom pods, lightly cracked

1–2 small fresh red chillies, chopped

2 tbsp ground cumin

½ tsp salt

½ tsp ground turmeric

2 tbsp cider vinegar

2 tbsp water

1 tbsp tomato purée

700 g/1 lb 9 oz boneless shoulder of pork, trimmed and cut into 5-cm/2-inch cubes

Put the mustard oil in a large frying pan or saucepan with a tight-fitting lid over a high heat until it smokes. Turn off the heat and leave the mustard oil to cool completely.

Reheat the oil over a medium-high heat. Add the onions and cook, stirring frequently, for 5–8 minutes until soft but not coloured.

Add the bay leaves, cloves, garlic, cardamom pods, chillies, cumin, salt, turmeric and 1 tablespoon of the vinegar to the onions and stir around. Stir in the water, then cover the pan and simmer for about 1 minute, or until the water is absorbed and the fat separates.

Dissolve the tomato purée in the remaining vinegar, then stir it into the pan. Add the pork and stir around.

Add just enough water to cover the pork and bring to the boil. Reduce the heat to its lowest level, cover the pan tightly and simmer for 40–60 minutes until the pork is tender.

If too much liquid remains in the pan when the pork is tender, use a slotted spoon to remove the pork from the pan and boil the liquid until it reduces to the required amount. Return the pork to the pan to heat through, then transfer to warmed dishes and serve.

Beef Madras

serves 4–6

1–2 dried red chillies

2 tsp ground coriander

2 tsp ground turmeric

1 tsp black mustard seeds

½ tsp ground ginger

¼ tsp ground pepper

140 g/5 oz creamed coconut, grated and dissolved in 300 ml/ 10 fl oz boiling water

55 g/2 oz ghee or 4 tbsp vegetable or groundnut oil

2 onions, chopped

3 large garlic cloves, chopped

700 g/1 lb 9 oz lean stewing steak, such as chuck, trimmed and cut into 5-cm/2-inch cubes

250 ml/9 fl oz beef stock

lemon juice

salt

sprigs of fresh coriander, to garnish

freshly cooked rice, to serve

Depending on how hot you want this dish to be, chop the chillies with or without any seeds. The more seeds you include, the hotter the dish will be. Put the chopped chilli and any seeds in a small bowl with the ground coriander, turmeric, mustard seeds, ginger and pepper and stir in a little of the coconut mixture to make a thin paste.

Heat the ghee in a large frying pan with a tight-fitting lid over a medium-high heat. Add the onions and garlic and cook for 5–8 minutes, stirring frequently, until the onions are golden brown. Add the spice paste and stir around for 2 minutes, or until the aromas are released.

Add the meat and stock and bring to the boil. Reduce the heat to its lowest level, cover tightly and simmer for 1½ hours, or until the beef is tender. Check occasionally that the meat isn't catching on the base of the pan and stir in a little extra water or stock, if necessary.

Uncover the pan and stir in the remaining coconut milk with the lemon juice and salt to taste. Bring to the boil, stirring, then reduce the heat again and simmer, still uncovered, until the sauce reduces slightly. Garnish with sprigs of coriander and serve with freshly cooked rice.

Balti Beef Curry

serves 4

2 tbsp ghee or vegetable oil

1 onion, thinly sliced

1 garlic clove, finely chopped

3-cm/1¼-inch piece fresh root ginger, grated

2 fresh red chillies, deseeded and finely chopped

450 g/1 lb rump steak, cut into thin strips

1 green pepper, deseeded and thinly sliced

1 yellow pepper, deseeded and thinly sliced

1 tsp ground cumin

1 tbsp garam masala

4 tomatoes, chopped

2 tbsp lemon juice

1 tbsp water

salt

chopped fresh coriander, to garnish

Heat 1 tablespoon of the ghee in a preheated wok or large, heavy-based frying pan. Add the onion and cook over a low heat, stirring occasionally, for 8–10 minutes, or until golden. Increase the heat to medium, add the garlic, ginger, chillies and steak and cook, stirring occasionally, for 5 minutes, or until the steak is browned all over. Remove with a slotted spoon, reserve and keep warm.

Add the remaining ghee to the wok, add the peppers and cook over a medium heat, stirring occasionally, for 4 minutes, or until softened. Stir in the cumin and garam masala and cook, stirring, for 1 minute.

Add the tomatoes, lemon juice and water, season to taste with salt and simmer, stirring constantly, for 3 minutes. Return the steak mixture to the wok and heat through. Transfer to a warmed serving dish, garnish with coriander and serve immediately.

Coconut Beef Curry

serves 4

1 tbsp ground coriander

1 tbsp ground cumin

3 tbsp mussaman curry paste

150 ml/5 fl oz water

75 g/2¾ oz creamed coconut

450 g/1 lb beef fillet, cut into strips

400 ml/14 fl oz coconut milk

50 g/1¾ oz unsalted peanuts, finely chopped

2 tbsp Thai fish sauce

1 tsp palm sugar or soft, light brown sugar

4 kaffir lime leaves

sprigs of fresh coriander, to garnish

freshly cooked rice with chopped fresh coriander, to serve

Combine the coriander, cumin and curry paste in a bowl. Pour the measured water into a saucepan, add the creamed coconut and heat until it has dissolved. Add the curry paste mixture and simmer for 1 minute.

Add the beef and simmer for 6–8 minutes, then add the coconut milk, peanuts, fish sauce and sugar. Simmer gently for 15–20 minutes, until the meat is tender.

Add the lime leaves and simmer for 1–2 minutes. Transfer to warmed serving dishes, garnish with sprigs of coriander and serve with freshly cooked rice with chopped coriander stirred through it.

Beef Korma with Almonds

serves 6

300 ml/10 fl oz vegetable oil

3 onions, finely chopped

1 kg/2 lb 4 oz lean beef, cubed

1½ tsp garam masala

1½ tsp ground coriander

1½ tsp finely chopped fresh root ginger

1½ tsp crushed fresh garlic

1 tsp salt

150 ml/5 fl oz natural yogurt

2 whole cloves

3 green cardamom pods

4 black peppercorns

600 ml/1 pint water

chapatis, to serve

to garnish

chopped blanched almonds

sliced fresh green chillies

chopped fresh coriander

Heat the oil in a large, heavy-based frying pan. Add the onions and stir-fry for 8–10 minutes, until golden. Remove half of the onions and reserve.

Add the meat to the remaining onions in the frying pan and stir-fry for 5 minutes. Remove the frying pan from the heat. Mix the garam masala, ground coriander, ginger, garlic, salt and yogurt together in a large bowl. Gradually add the meat to the yogurt and spice mixture and mix to coat the meat on all sides. Place the meat mixture in the frying pan, return to the heat, and stir-fry for 5–7 minutes, or until the mixture is nearly brown.

Add the cloves, cardamom pods and peppercorns. Add the water, reduce the heat, cover and simmer for 45–60 minutes. If the water has completely evaporated, but the meat is still not tender enough, add another 300 ml/10 fl oz water and cook for a further 10–15 minutes, stirring occasionally. Transfer to serving dishes and garnish with the reserved onions, chopped almonds, chillies and fresh coriander. Serve with chapatis.

Beef Dhansak

serves 6

2 tbsp ghee or vegetable oil

2 onions, chopped

3 garlic cloves, finely chopped

2 tsp ground coriander

2 tsp ground cumin

2 tsp garam masala

1 tsp ground turmeric

450 g/1 lb courgettes, peeled and chopped, or bitter gourd or pumpkin, peeled, deseeded and chopped

1 aubergine, peeled and chopped

4 curry leaves

225 g/8 oz masoor dal

1 litre/1¾ pints water

1 kg/2 lb 4 oz stewing or braising steak, diced

salt

fresh coriander leaves, to garnish

Heat the ghee in a large, heavy-based saucepan. Add the onions and garlic and cook over a low heat, stirring occasionally, for 8–10 minutes, or until light golden. Stir in the ground coriander, cumin, garam masala and turmeric and cook, stirring constantly, for 2 minutes.

Add the courgettes, aubergine, curry leaves, masoor dal and water. Bring to the boil, then reduce the heat, cover and simmer for 30 minutes, or until the vegetables are tender. Remove the saucepan from the heat and leave to cool slightly. Transfer the mixture to a food processor, in batches if necessary, and process until smooth. Return the mixture to the saucepan and season to taste with salt.

Add the steak to the saucepan and bring to the boil. Reduce the heat, cover and simmer for 1¼ hours. Remove the lid and continue to simmer for a further 30 minutes, or until the sauce is thick and the steak is tender. Serve garnished with coriander leaves.

Fish & Seafood

Mixed Seafood Curry

serves 4

1 tbsp vegetable or groundnut oil

3 shallots, finely chopped

2.5-cm/1-inch piece fresh galangal, peeled and thinly sliced

2 garlic cloves, finely chopped

400 ml/14 fl oz coconut milk

2 lemon grass stalks, snapped in half

4 tbsp Thai fish sauce

2 tbsp chilli sauce

225 g/8 oz raw tiger prawns, peeled and deveined

225 g/8 oz baby squid, cleaned and thickly sliced

225 g/8 oz salmon fillet, skinned and cut into chunks

175 g/6 oz tuna steak, cut into chunks

225 g/8 oz fresh mussels, scrubbed and debearded

fresh Chinese chives, to garnish

freshly cooked rice, to serve

Heat the oil in a large wok with a tight-fitting lid and stir-fry the shallots, galangal and garlic for 1–2 minutes, until they start to soften. Add the coconut milk, lemon grass, fish sauce and chilli sauce. Bring to the boil, lower the heat and simmer for 1–2 minutes.

Add the prawns, squid, salmon and tuna and simmer for 3–4 minutes, until the prawns have turned pink and the fish is cooked.

Discard any mussels with broken shells or any that refuse to close when tapped with a knife. Add the remaining mussels to the wok and cover with a lid. Simmer for 1–2 minutes, until they have opened. Discard any mussels that remain closed. Garnish with Chinese chives and serve immediately with freshly cooked rice.

Fish Curry with Rice Noodles

serves 4

2 tbsp vegetable or groundnut oil

1 large onion, chopped

2 garlic cloves, chopped

85 g/3 oz button mushrooms

225 g/8 oz monkfish, cut into 2.5-cm/1-inch cubes

225 g/8 oz salmon fillets, cut into 2.5-cm/1-inch cubes

225 g/8 oz cod, cut into 2.5-cm/1-inch cubes

2 tbsp Thai red curry paste

400 g/14 oz coconut milk

handful of fresh coriander, chopped

1 tsp palm sugar or soft, light brown sugar

1 tsp Thai fish sauce

115 g/4 oz rice noodles

3 spring onions, chopped

55 g/2 oz beansprouts

a few fresh Thai basil leaves

Heat the oil in a wok or large frying pan and gently fry the onion, garlic and mushrooms until softened but not browned.

Add the fish, curry paste and coconut milk and bring gently to the boil. Simmer for 2–3 minutes before adding the coriander, sugar and fish sauce. Keep warm.

Meanwhile, soak the noodles for 3–4 minutes (or according to the packet instructions) or until tender and drain well through a colander. Put the colander and noodles over a saucepan of simmering water. Add the spring onions, beansprouts and basil and steam on top of the noodles for 1–2 minutes or until just wilted.

Pile the noodles into warmed serving dishes, top with the fish curry and serve immediately.

Fish in Coconut

serves 4

2 tbsp vegetable or groundnut oil

6 spring onions, coarsely chopped

2.5-cm/1-inch piece fresh root ginger, grated

2–3 tbsp Thai red curry paste

400 ml/14 fl oz coconut milk

150 ml/5 fl oz fish stock

4 kaffir lime leaves

1 lemon grass stalk, broken in half

350 g/12 oz white fish fillets, skinned and cut into chunks

225 g/8 oz squid rings and tentacles

225 g/8 oz large cooked peeled prawns

1 tbsp fish sauce

2 tbsp Thai soy sauce

4 tbsp snipped fresh Chinese chives

Heat the oil in a wok or large frying pan and stir-fry the spring onions and ginger for 1–2 minutes. Add the curry paste and stir-fry for 1–2 minutes.

Add the coconut milk, fish stock, lime leaves and lemon grass. Bring to the boil, then lower the heat and simmer for 1 minute.

Add the fish, squid and prawns and simmer for 2–3 minutes, until the fish is cooked. Add the fish sauce and soy sauce and stir in the chives. Serve immediately.

Goan-style Seafood Curry

serves 4–6

3 tbsp vegetable or groundnut oil

1 tbsp black mustard seeds

12 fresh curry leaves or 1 tbsp dried

6 shallots, finely chopped

1 garlic clove, crushed

1 tsp ground turmeric

½ tsp ground coriander

¼–½ tsp chilli powder

140 g/5 oz creamed coconut, grated and dissolved in 300 ml/ 10 fl oz boiling water

500 g/1 lb 2 oz skinless, boneless white fish, such as monkfish or cod, cut into large chunks

450 g/1 lb large raw prawns, peeled and deveined

finely grated rind and juice of 1 lime

salt

lime wedges, to serve

Heat the oil in a wok or large frying pan over a high heat. Add the mustard seeds and stir them around for about 1 minute, or until they pop. Stir in the curry leaves.

Add the shallots and garlic and stir for about 5 minutes, or until the shallots are golden. Stir in the turmeric, coriander and chilli powder and continue stirring for about 30 seconds.

Add the dissolved creamed coconut. Bring to the boil, then reduce the heat to medium and stir for about 2 minutes.

Reduce the heat to low, add the fish and simmer for 1 minute, spooning the sauce over the fish and very gently stirring it around. Add the prawns and continue to simmer for 4–5 minutes longer until the fish flakes easily and the prawns turn pink and curl.

Add half the lime juice, then taste and add more lime juice and salt to taste. Sprinkle with the lime rind and serve with lime wedges.

Bengali-style Fish

serves 4–8

1 tsp ground turmeric

1 tsp salt

1 kg/2 lb 4 oz cod fillet, skinned and cut into pieces

6 tbsp mustard oil

4 fresh green chillies

1 tsp finely chopped fresh root ginger

1 tsp crushed garlic

2 onions, finely chopped

2 tomatoes, finely chopped

450 ml/16 fl oz water

chopped fresh coriander, to garnish

naan bread, to serve

Mix the turmeric and salt together in a small bowl, then spoon the mixture over the fish pieces.

Heat the mustard oil in a large, heavy-based frying pan. Add the fish and fry until pale yellow. Remove the fish with a slotted spoon and reserve.

Place the chillies, ginger, garlic, onions and tomatoes in a mortar and grind with a pestle to make a paste. Alternatively, place the ingredients in a food processor and process until smooth.

Transfer the spice paste to a clean frying pan and dry-fry until golden brown.

Remove the frying pan from the heat and place the fish pieces in the paste without breaking up the fish. Return the frying pan to the heat, add the water and cook over a medium heat for 15–20 minutes. Transfer to a warmed serving dish, garnish with chopped coriander and serve with naan bread.

Balti Fish Curry

serves 4–6

900 g/2 lb thick fish fillets, such as monkfish, grey mullet, cod or haddock, rinsed and cut into large chunks

2 bay leaves, torn

140 g/5 oz ghee or 150 ml/5 fl oz vegetable or groundnut oil

2 large onions, chopped

½ tbsp salt

150 ml/5 fl oz water

sprigs of fresh coriander, to garnish

for the marinade

½ tbsp garlic and ginger paste

1 fresh green chilli, deseeded and chopped

1 tsp ground coriander

1 tsp ground cumin

½ tsp ground turmeric

½ tsp chilli powder

salt

1 tbsp water

To make the marinade, mix the garlic and ginger paste, green chilli, ground coriander, cumin, turmeric and chilli powder together with salt to taste in a large bowl. Gradually stir in the water to form a thin paste. Add the fish chunks and smear with the marinade. Tuck the bay leaves underneath and leave to marinate in the refrigerator for at least 30 minutes, or up to 4 hours.

When you are ready to cook the fish, remove from the refrigerator 15 minutes in advance. Heat the ghee in a wok or large frying pan over a medium-high heat. Add the onions, sprinkle with the salt and cook, stirring frequently, for 8 minutes, or until very soft and golden.

Gently add the fish, bay leaves, and marinade to the pan and stir in the water. Bring to the boil, then immediately reduce the heat and cook the fish for 4–5 minutes, spooning the sauce over the fish and carefully moving the chunks around, until they are cooked through and flake easily. Transfer to warmed dishes and serve garnished with sprigs of coriander.

Fish Curry

serves 4

juice of 1 lime

4 tbsp Thai fish sauce

2 tbsp Thai soy sauce

1 fresh red chilli, deseeded and chopped

350 g/12 oz monkfish fillet, cut into cubes

350 g/12 oz salmon fillet, skinned and cut into cubes

400 ml/14 fl oz coconut milk

3 kaffir lime leaves

1 tbsp Thai red curry paste

1 lemon grass stalk (white part only), finely chopped

225 g/8 oz jasmine rice, boiled

4 tbsp chopped fresh coriander

Combine the lime juice, 2 tablespoons of the fish sauce and the soy sauce in a shallow, non-metallic dish. Add the chilli and the fish, stir to coat, cover with clingfilm and chill for 1–2 hours, or overnight.

Bring the coconut milk to the boil in a saucepan and add the lime leaves, curry paste, the remaining fish sauce and the lemon grass. Simmer gently for 10–15 minutes.

Add the fish and the marinade and simmer gently for 4–5 minutes, until the fish is cooked. Serve hot with freshly cooked rice with chopped coriander stirred through it.

Mixed Fish & Coconut Curry

serves 4

2 tbsp groundnut or vegetable oil

6 spring onions, cut into 2.5-cm/1-inch lengths

1 large carrot, peeled and cut into matchsticks

55 g/2 oz green beans, trimmed and cut into short lengths

2 tbsp Thai red curry paste

700 ml/1¼ pints coconut milk

225 g/8 oz skinned white fish fillet, such as cod or coley, cut into 2.5-cm/ 1-inch cubes

225 g/8 oz squid, cleaned and cut into thick rings

225 g/8 oz large raw prawns, peeled and deveined

55 g/2 oz fresh beansprouts

115 g/4 oz dried rice noodles, cooked and drained

handful of fresh coriander, chopped

handful of fresh Thai basil leaves, to garnish

Heat the oil in a preheated wok, add the spring onions, carrot and green beans and stir-fry over a medium-high heat for 2–3 minutes until starting to soften.

Stir in the curry paste, then add the coconut milk. Bring gently to the boil, stirring occasionally, then reduce the heat and simmer for 2–3 minutes. Add all the fish, squid, prawns and beansprouts and simmer for 2–3 minutes until just cooked through and the prawns have turned pink.

Stir in the cooked noodles and coriander and cook for 1 minute. Serve immediately, scattered with the basil.

Thai Green Fish Curry

serves 4

2 tbsp vegetable oil

1 garlic clove, chopped

2 tbsp Thai green curry paste

1 small aubergine, diced

125 ml/4 fl oz coconut milk

2 tbsp Thai fish sauce

1 tsp sugar

225 g/8 oz firm white fish fillets, cut into pieces

125 ml/4 fl oz fish stock

2 kaffir lime leaves, finely shredded

about 15 fresh Thai basil leaves

sprigs of fresh dill, to garnish

Heat the vegetable oil in a large frying pan or preheated wok over a medium heat until almost smoking. Add the garlic and cook until golden. Add the curry paste and stir-fry a few seconds before adding the aubergine. Stir-fry for about 4–5 minutes until softened.

Add the coconut milk, bring to the boil and stir until it thickens and curdles slightly. Add the fish sauce and sugar to the frying pan and stir well.

Add the fish pieces and stock. Simmer for 3–4 minutes, stirring occasionally, until the fish is just tender. Add the lime leaves and basil, then cook for a further 1 minute. Transfer to a warmed serving dish and garnish with a few sprigs of fresh dill. Serve immediately.

Cod Curry

serves 4

1 tbsp vegetable oil

1 small onion, chopped

2 garlic cloves, chopped

2.5-cm/1-inch piece fresh
root ginger, coarsely
chopped

2 large ripe tomatoes,
peeled and coarsely
chopped

150 ml/5 fl oz fish stock

1 tbsp medium curry paste

1 tsp ground coriander

400 g/14 oz canned
chickpeas, drained and
rinsed

750 g/1 lb 10 oz cod fillet,
cut into large chunks

4 tbsp chopped fresh
coriander

4 tbsp thick yogurt

salt and pepper

freshly cooked rice,
to serve

Heat the oil in a large saucepan over a low heat. Add the onion, garlic and ginger and cook for 4–5 minutes until softened. Remove from the heat. Put the onion mixture into a food processor or blender with the tomatoes and fish stock and process until smooth.

Return to the saucepan with the curry paste, ground coriander and chickpeas. Mix together well, then simmer gently for 15 minutes until thickened.

Add the pieces of fish and return to a simmer. Cook for 5 minutes until the fish is just tender. Remove from the heat and leave to stand for 2–3 minutes.

Stir in the coriander and yogurt. Season to taste with salt and pepper and serve with freshly cooked rice.

Curried Noodles with Prawns

serves 4

1 tbsp vegetable or groundnut oil

3 shallots, chopped

1 fresh red chilli, deseeded and chopped

1 tbsp Thai red curry paste

1 lemon grass stalk (white part only), finely chopped

225 g/8 oz cooked peeled prawns

400 g/14 oz canned straw mushrooms, drained

2 tbsp Thai fish sauce

2 tbsp Thai soy sauce

225 g/8 oz fresh egg noodles

chopped fresh coriander, to garnish

Heat the oil in a wok and stir-fry the shallots and chilli for 2–3 minutes. Add the curry paste and lemon grass and stir-fry for 2–3 minutes.

Add the prawns, mushrooms, fish sauce and soy sauce and stir well to mix.

Meanwhile, cook the noodles in boiling water for 3–4 minutes, drain and transfer to warmed plates.

Top the noodles with the prawn curry, sprinkle over the coriander and serve immediately.

Prawn Biryani

serves 8

1 tsp saffron strands

55 ml/2 fl oz tepid water

2 shallots, coarsely chopped

3 garlic cloves, crushed

1 tsp chopped fresh root ginger

2 tsp coriander seeds

½ tsp black peppercorns

2 cloves

seeds from 2 green cardamom pods

½ cinnamon stick

1 tsp ground turmeric

1 green chilli, chopped

½ tsp salt

2 tbsp ghee

1 tsp black mustard seeds

500 g/1 lb 2 oz raw tiger prawns, peeled and deveined

300 ml/10 fl oz coconut milk

300 ml/10 fl oz natural yogurt

to serve/garnish

freshly cooked rice

toasted flaked almonds

sliced spring onion

sprigs of fresh coriander

Soak the saffron in the tepid water for 10 minutes. Put the shallots, garlic, ginger, coriander seeds, peppercorns, cloves, cardamom seeds, cinnamon stick, turmeric, chilli and salt into a spice grinder or mortar and pestle and grind to a paste.

Heat the ghee in a saucepan and add the mustard seeds. When they start to pop, add the prawns and stir over a high heat for 1 minute. Stir in the spice mix, then the coconut milk and yogurt. Simmer for 20 minutes.

Spoon the prawn mixture into serving bowls. Top with the freshly cooked rice and drizzle over the saffron water. Serve garnished with the flaked almonds, spring onion and sprigs of coriander.

Prawn Masala

serves 4

2 fresh red chillies, deseeded and chopped

2 garlic cloves, chopped

½ onion, chopped

2.5-cm/1-inch piece fresh root ginger, chopped

1 tsp ground turmeric

1 tsp ground cumin

1 tsp garam masala

½ tsp sugar

½ tsp pepper

300 ml/10 fl oz natural yogurt

2 tbsp chopped fresh coriander

500 g/1 lb 2 oz raw tiger prawns, peeled, deveined and tails left intact

lime wedges, to serve

If you are using wooden skewers, soak them in cold water for 30 minutes.

Put the chillies into a food processor with the garlic, onion, ginger, turmeric, cumin, garam masala, sugar, pepper and yogurt. Process until smooth, then transfer to a large, shallow dish. Stir in the coriander. Thread the prawns onto metal kebab skewers or pre-soaked wooden skewers, leaving a small space at either end. Transfer them to the dish and turn in the mixture until thoroughly coated. Cover with clingfilm and refrigerate for 1–1½ hours.

Preheat the grill. Remove from the refrigerator and arrange the skewers on a grill rack. Cook under a preheated medium grill, turning and basting with the marinade, for 4 minutes, until sizzling and cooked through.

Serve hot with lime wedges for squeezing over.

Prawns in Coconut Milk

serves 4

4 onions

4 tbsp ghee or vegetable oil

1 tsp garam masala

1 tsp ground turmeric

1 cinnamon stick

2 cardamom pods, lightly crushed

½ tsp chilli powder

2 whole cloves

2 bay leaves

400 ml/14 fl oz coconut milk

1 tsp sugar

500 g/1 lb 2 oz raw tiger prawns, peeled and deveined

salt

pilau rice, to serve

Finely chop 2 of the onions and grate the other 2. Heat the ghee in a large, heavy-based frying pan. Add the garam masala and cook over a low heat, stirring constantly, for 1 minute, or until its aroma is released. Add the chopped onions and cook, stirring occasionally, for 10 minutes, or until golden.

Stir in the grated onions, turmeric, cinnamon, cardamom pods, chilli powder, cloves and bay leaves and cook, stirring constantly, for 5 minutes. Stir in half the coconut milk and the sugar and season to taste with salt. Add the prawns and cook, stirring frequently for 8 minutes, or until they have changed colour.

Stir in the remaining coconut milk and bring to the boil. Taste and adjust the seasoning, if necessary, and serve immediately with pilau rice.

Bengali Coriander Prawns

serves 4

4 fresh green chillies, deseeded

4 spring onions, chopped

3 garlic cloves

2.5-cm/1-inch piece fresh root ginger, chopped

2 tsp sunflower oil

4 tbsp mustard oil or vegetable oil

1 tbsp ground coriander

1 tsp mustard seeds, crushed

175 ml/6 fl oz coconut milk

500 g/1 lb 2 oz raw tiger prawns, peeled and deveined

115 g/4 oz chopped fresh coriander, plus extra leaves to garnish

salt

freshly cooked rice, to serve

lemon halves, to garnish

Place the chillies, spring onions, garlic, ginger and sunflower oil in a food processor and process to a smooth paste. Heat the mustard oil in a large, heavy-based frying pan. Add the spice paste and cook over a low heat, stirring constantly, for 2 minutes.

Add the ground coriander, mustard seeds and coconut milk and bring to the boil, stirring constantly. Reduce the heat and simmer for 5 minutes.

Stir in the prawns and simmer for a further 6–8 minutes, or until they have changed colour. Season with salt to taste, stir in the chopped coriander and serve immediately with freshly cooked rice. Garnish with lemon halves and a few coriander leaves.

Tandoori Prawns

serves 4

4 tbsp natural yogurt

2 fresh green chillies, deseeded and chopped

½ tbsp garlic and ginger paste

seeds from 4 green cardamom pods

2 tsp ground cumin

1 tsp tomato purée

¼ tsp ground turmeric

¼ tsp salt

pinch of chilli powder, ideally Kashmiri chilli powder

24 raw tiger prawns, thawed if frozen, peeled, deveined and tails left intact

oil, for greasing

Put the yogurt, chillies and garlic and ginger paste in a small food processor or spice grinder and process to a smooth paste. Transfer the paste to a large non-metallic bowl and stir in the cardamom seeds, cumin, tomato purée, turmeric, salt and chilli powder.

Add the prawns to the bowl and use your hands to make sure they are coated with the yogurt marinade. Cover the bowl with clingfilm and chill for at least 30 minutes, or up to 4 hours.

When you are ready to cook, heat a large griddle or frying pan over a high heat until a few drops of water 'dance' when they hit the surface. Use crumpled kitchen paper or a pastry brush to very lightly grease the hot pan with oil.

Use tongs to lift the prawns out of the marinade, letting the excess drip back into the bowl, then place the prawns on the griddle and leave them to cook for 2 minutes. Flip the prawns over and cook for a further 1–2 minutes until they turn pink, curl and are opaque all the way through when you cut one. Serve immediately.

Prawns with Spring Onions & Mushrooms

serves 4

2 tbsp vegetable or groundnut oil

1 bunch of spring onions, chopped

2 garlic cloves, finely chopped

175 g/6 oz creamed coconut, coarsely chopped

2 tbsp Thai red curry paste

450 ml/16 fl oz fish stock

2 tbsp Thai fish sauce

2 tbsp Thai soy sauce

6 sprigs of fresh Thai basil

400 g/14 oz canned straw mushrooms, drained

350 g/12 oz large cooked peeled prawns

freshly cooked jasmine rice, to serve

Heat the oil in a wok and stir-fry the spring onions and garlic for 2–3 minutes. Add the creamed coconut, curry paste and stock and heat gently until the coconut has dissolved.

Stir in the fish sauce and soy sauce, then add the basil, mushrooms and prawns. Gradually bring to the boil and serve immediately with freshly cooked jasmine rice.

Prawn & Pineapple Tikka

makes 4

1 tsp cumin seeds

1 tsp coriander seeds

½ tsp fennel seeds

½ tsp yellow mustard seeds

¼ tsp fenugreek seeds

¼ tsp nigella seeds

pinch of chilli powder

pinch of salt

2 tbsp lemon or pineapple juice

12 raw tiger prawns, peeled, deveined and tails left intact

12 bite-sized wedges of fresh or well-drained canned pineapple

chopped fresh coriander, to garnish

If you are using wooden skewers, rather than metal ones, soak them in cold water for 30 minutes.

Dry-fry the cumin, coriander, fennel, mustard, fenugreek and nigella seeds in a hot frying pan over a high heat, stirring them around constantly, until you can smell the aroma of the spices. Immediately tip the spices out of the pan so they do not burn.

Put the spices in a spice grinder or mortar, add the chilli powder and salt and grind to a fine powder. Transfer to a non-metallic bowl and stir in the lemon juice.

Add the prawns to the bowl and stir them around so they are well coated, then set aside to marinate for 10 minutes. Meanwhile, preheat the grill to high.

Thread 3 prawns and 3 pineapple wedges alternately onto each metal or pre-soaked wooden skewer. Grill about 10 cm/4 inches from the heat for 2 minutes on each side, brushing with any leftover marinade, until the prawns turn pink and are cooked through.

Serve the prawns and pineapple wedges on a plate with plenty of coriander sprinkled over.

Vegetable Dishes

Vegetable Curry

serves 4

1 aubergine

225 g/8 oz turnips

350 g/12 oz new potatoes

225 g/8 oz cauliflower

225 g/8 oz button
mushrooms

1 large onion

3 carrots

6 tbsp ghee

2 garlic cloves, crushed

4 tsp finely chopped fresh
root ginger

1–2 fresh green chillies,
deseeded and chopped

1 tbsp paprika

2 tsp ground coriander

1 tbsp mild or medium
curry powder

450 ml/16 fl oz vegetable
stock

400 g/14 oz canned
chopped tomatoes

1 green pepper, deseeded
and sliced

1 tbsp cornflour

150 ml/5 fl oz coconut milk

2–3 tbsp ground almonds

salt and pepper

sprigs of fresh coriander,
to garnish

freshly cooked rice,
to serve

Cut the aubergine, turnips and potatoes into 1-cm/½-inch cubes. Divide the cauliflower into small florets. Leave the button mushrooms whole or slice them thickly, if preferred. Slice the onion and carrots.

Heat the ghee in a large, heavy-based saucepan. Add the onion, turnip, potatoes and cauliflower and cook over a low heat, stirring frequently, for 3 minutes. Add the garlic, ginger, chillies, paprika, ground coriander and curry powder and cook, stirring, for 1 minute.

Add the stock, tomatoes, aubergine and mushrooms, and season to taste with salt. Cover and simmer, stirring occasionally, for 30 minutes, or until tender. Add the green pepper and carrots, cover and cook for a further 5 minutes.

Place the cornflour and coconut milk in a bowl, mix into a smooth paste and stir into the vegetable mixture. Add the ground almonds and simmer, stirring constantly, for 2 minutes. Taste and adjust the seasoning, adding salt and pepper if necessary. Transfer to warmed serving plates, garnish with sprigs of coriander and serve immediately with freshly cooked rice.

Chunky Potato & Spinach Curry

serves 4

4 tomatoes

2 tbsp groundnut or vegetable oil

2 onions, cut into thick wedges

2.5-cm/1-inch piece fresh root ginger, peeled and finely chopped

1 garlic clove, chopped

2 tbsp ground coriander

450 g/1 lb potatoes, cut into chunks

600 ml/1 pint vegetable stock

1 tbsp Thai red curry paste

225 g/8 oz spinach leaves

Put the tomatoes in a heatproof bowl and cover with boiling water. Leave for 2–3 minutes, then plunge into cold water and peel off the skins. Cut each tomato into quarters and remove and discard the seeds and central core. Set aside.

Heat the oil in a preheated wok, add the onions, ginger and garlic and stir-fry over a medium-high heat for 2–3 minutes until starting to soften. Add the coriander and potatoes and stir-fry for 2–3 minutes. Add the stock and curry paste and bring to the boil, stirring occasionally. Reduce the heat and simmer gently for 10–15 minutes until the potatoes are tender.

Add the spinach and the tomato quarters and cook, stirring, for 1 minute, or until the spinach has wilted. Serve immediately

Vegetable Korma

serves 4

4 tbsp ghee or vegetable oil

2 onions, chopped

2 garlic cloves, chopped

1 fresh red chilli, chopped

1 tbsp grated fresh root ginger

2 tomatoes, peeled and chopped

1 orange pepper, deseeded and cut into small pieces

1 large potato, cut into chunks

200 g/7 oz cauliflower florets

½ tsp salt

1 tsp ground turmeric

1 tsp ground cumin

1 tsp ground coriander

1 tsp garam masala

200 ml/7 fl oz vegetable stock or water

150 ml/5 fl oz natural yogurt

150 ml/5 fl oz single cream

25 g/1 oz fresh coriander, chopped

freshly cooked rice, to serve

Heat the ghee in a large saucepan over a medium heat, add the onions and garlic and cook, stirring, for 3 minutes. Add the chilli and ginger and cook for a further 4 minutes. Add the tomatoes, orange pepper, potato, cauliflower, salt and spices and cook, stirring, for a further 3 minutes. Stir in the stock and bring to the boil. Reduce the heat and simmer for 25 minutes.

Stir in the yogurt and cream and cook, stirring, for a further 5 minutes. Add the fresh coriander and heat through.

Serve with freshly cooked rice.

Carrot & Pumpkin Curry

serves 4

150 ml/5 fl oz vegetable stock

2.5-cm/1-inch piece fresh galangal, sliced

2 garlic cloves, chopped

1 lemon grass stalk (white part only), finely chopped

2 fresh red chillies, deseeded and chopped

4 carrots, peeled and cut into chunks

225 g/8 oz pumpkin, peeled, deseeded and cut into cubes

2 tbsp vegetable or groundnut oil

2 shallots, finely chopped

3 tbsp Thai yellow curry paste

400 ml/14 fl oz coconut milk

4–6 sprigs of fresh Thai basil

25 g/1 oz toasted pumpkin seeds, to garnish

Pour the stock into a large saucepan and bring to the boil. Add the galangal, half the garlic, the lemon grass and chillies and simmer for 5 minutes. Add the carrots and pumpkin and simmer for 5–6 minutes, until tender.

Meanwhile, heat the oil in a wok or frying pan and stir-fry the shallots and the remaining garlic for 2–3 minutes. Add the curry paste and stir-fry for 1–2 minutes.

Stir the shallot mixture into the saucepan and add the coconut milk and Thai basil. Simmer for 2–3 minutes. Serve hot, sprinkled with the toasted pumpkin seeds.

Chilli-yogurt Mushrooms

serves 4–6

55 g/2 oz ghee or 4 tbsp vegetable or groundnut oil

2 large onions, chopped

4 large garlic cloves, crushed

400 g/14 oz canned chopped tomatoes

1 tsp ground turmeric

1 tsp garam masala

½ tsp chilli powder

750 g/1 lb 10 oz chestnut mushrooms, thickly sliced

pinch of sugar

125 ml/4 fl oz natural yogurt

salt and pepper

chopped fresh coriander, to garnish

freshly cooked rice, to serve

Heat the ghee in a wok or large frying pan over a medium-high heat. Add the onions and cook, stirring frequently, for 5–8 minutes until golden. Stir in the garlic and cook for a further 2 minutes.

Add the tomatoes and mix around. Stir in the turmeric, garam masala and chilli powder and continue cooking for a further 3 minutes.

Add the mushrooms, sugar and salt to taste and cook for about 8 minutes, until the mushrooms have given off their liquid and are soft and tender.

Turn off the heat, then stir in the yogurt, a little at a time, beating vigorously to prevent it curdling. Taste and adjust the seasoning, adding salt and pepper if necessary. Sprinkle with coriander and serve with freshly cooked rice.

Butternut Squash Curry

serves 4

2 tbsp groundnut or vegetable oil

1 tsp cumin seeds

2 red onions, sliced

2 celery sticks, sliced

1 large butternut squash, peeled, deseeded and cut into chunks

2 tbsp Thai green curry paste

300 ml/10 fl oz vegetable stock

2 fresh kaffir lime leaves

55 g/2 oz fresh beansprouts

handful of fresh coriander, chopped, to garnish

freshly cooked rice, to serve

Heat the oil in a preheated wok, add the cumin seeds and stir-fry over a medium-high heat for 2–3 minutes until starting to pop. Add the onions and celery and stir-fry for 2–3 minutes. Add the squash and stir-fry for 3–4 minutes. Add the curry paste, stock and lime leaves and bring to the boil, stirring occasionally.

Reduce the heat and simmer gently for 3–4 minutes until the squash is tender. Add the beansprouts and cook for a further 1–2 minutes until hot but still crunchy. Scatter the coriander over the curry and serve immediately with freshly cooked rice.

Pumpkin Curry

serves 4

150 ml/5 fl oz vegetable oil

2 onions, sliced

½ tsp white cumin seeds

450 g/1 lb pumpkin, cubed

1 tsp aamchoor (dried mango powder)

1 tsp finely chopped fresh root ginger

1 tsp crushed fresh garlic

1 tsp crushed red chilli

½ tsp salt

300 ml/10 fl oz water

chapatis, to serve

Heat the oil in a large, heavy-based frying pan. Add the onions and cumin seeds and cook, stirring occasionally, for 5–6 minutes, until a light golden brown colour.

Add the pumpkin to the frying pan and stir-fry for 3–5 minutes over a low heat.

Mix the aamchoor, ginger, garlic, chilli and salt together in a bowl. Add to the onion and pumpkin mixture in the pan and stir well.

Add the water, cover and cook over a low heat for 10–15 minutes, stirring occasionally. Transfer the curry to serving plates and serve hot with chapatis.

Aubergine & Bean Curry

serves 4

2 tbsp vegetable or groundnut oil

1 onion, chopped

2 garlic cloves, crushed

2 fresh red chillies, deseeded and chopped

1 tbsp Thai red curry paste

1 large aubergine, cut into chunks

115 g/4 oz pea or small aubergines

115 g/4 oz baby broad beans

115 g/4 oz fine French beans

300 ml/10 fl oz vegetable stock

55 g/2 oz creamed coconut, chopped

3 tbsp Thai soy sauce

1 tsp palm sugar or soft, light brown sugar

3 kaffir lime leaves, torn coarsely

4 tbsp chopped fresh coriander

Heat the oil in a wok or large frying pan and cook the onion, garlic and chillies for 1–2 minutes. Stir in the curry paste and cook for 1–2 minutes.

Add the aubergines and cook for 3–4 minutes, until starting to soften. (You may need to add a little more oil as aubergines soak it up quickly.) Add all the beans and stir-fry for 2 minutes.

Pour in the stock and add the creamed coconut, soy sauce, sugar and lime leaves. Bring gently to the boil and cook until the coconut has dissolved. Stir in the coriander and serve hot.

Cauliflower & Sweet Potato Curry

serves 4

4 tbsp ghee or vegetable oil

2 onions, finely chopped

1 tsp panch phoran

1 cauliflower, broken into small florets

350 g/12 oz sweet potatoes, diced

2 fresh green chillies, deseeded and finely chopped

1 tsp ginger paste

2 tsp paprika

1½ tsp ground cumin

1 tsp ground turmeric

½ tsp chilli powder

3 tomatoes, quartered

225 g/8 oz fresh or frozen peas

3 tbsp natural yogurt

225 ml/8 fl oz vegetable stock or water

1 tsp garam masala

salt

sprigs of fresh coriander, to garnish

Heat the ghee in a large, heavy-based frying pan. Add the onions and panch phoran and cook over a low heat, stirring frequently, for 10 minutes, or until the onions are golden. Add the cauliflower, sweet potatoes and chillies and cook, stirring frequently, for 3 minutes.

Stir in the ginger paste, paprika, cumin, turmeric and chilli powder and cook, stirring constantly, for 3 minutes. Add the tomatoes and peas and stir in the yogurt and stock. Season with salt to taste, cover and simmer for 20 minutes, or until the vegetables are tender.

Sprinkle the garam masala over the curry, transfer to a warmed serving dish and serve immediately, garnished with sprigs of fresh coriander.

Courgette & Cashew Nut Curry

serves 4

2 tbsp vegetable or groundnut oil

6 spring onions, chopped

2 garlic cloves, chopped

2 fresh green chillies, deseeded and chopped

450 g/1 lb courgettes, cut into thick slices

115 g/4 oz shiitake mushrooms, halved

55 g/2 oz beansprouts

85 g/3 oz cashew nuts, toasted or dry-fried

a few Chinese chives, snipped

4 tbsp Thai soy sauce

1 tsp Thai fish sauce

freshly cooked noodles, to serve

Heat the oil in a wok or large frying pan and cook the spring onions, garlic and chillies for 1–2 minutes, until softened but not browned.

Add the courgettes and mushrooms and cook for 2–3 minutes until tender.

Add the beansprouts, cashew nuts, chives, soy sauce and fish sauce and stir-fry for 1–2 minutes.

Serve hot with freshly cooked noodles.

Tofu & Vegetable Curry

serves 4

vegetable or groundnut oil, for deep-frying

225 g/8 oz firm tofu, drained and cut into cubes

2 tbsp vegetable or groundnut oil

2 onions, chopped

2 garlic cloves, chopped

1 fresh red chilli, deseeded and sliced

3 celery sticks, diagonally sliced

225 g/8 oz mushrooms, thickly sliced

115 g/4 oz baby corn cobs, cut in half

1 red pepper, deseeded and cut into strips

3 tbsp Thai red curry paste

400 ml/14 fl oz coconut milk

1 tsp palm sugar or soft, light brown sugar

2 tbsp Thai soy sauce

225 g/8 oz baby spinach leaves

Heat the oil for deep-frying in a preheated wok or a deep saucepan or deep-fat fryer to 180–190°C/350–375°F, or until a cube of bread browns in 30 seconds. Add the tofu cubes, in batches, and cook for 4–5 minutes until crisp and brown all over. Remove with a slotted spoon and drain on kitchen paper.

Heat the 2 tablespoons of oil in a wok or frying pan and stir-fry the onions, garlic and chilli for 1–2 minutes, until they start to soften. Add the celery, mushrooms, corn cobs and red pepper and stir-fry for 3–4 minutes, until they soften.

Stir in the curry paste and coconut milk and gradually bring to the boil. Add the sugar and soy sauce and then the spinach. Cook, stirring constantly, until the spinach has wilted. Serve immediately, topped with the tofu.

Aubergine Curry

serves 2

groundnut or vegetable oil,
for deep-frying

2 aubergines, cut into
2-cm/$\frac{3}{4}$-inch cubes

2 tbsp groundnut or
vegetable oil

1 bunch of spring onions,
coarsely chopped

2 garlic cloves, chopped

2 red peppers, deseeded
and cut into 2-cm/$\frac{3}{4}$-inch
squares

3 courgettes, thickly sliced

400 ml/14 fl oz coconut milk

2 tbsp Thai red curry paste

large handful of fresh
coriander, chopped, plus
extra sprigs to garnish

Heat the oil for deep-frying in a preheated wok or a deep saucepan or deep-fat fryer to 180–190°C/350–375°F, or until a cube of bread browns in 30 seconds. Add the aubergine cubes, in batches, and cook for 45 seconds–1 minute until crisp and brown all over. Remove with a slotted spoon and drain on kitchen paper.

Heat the 2 tablespoons of oil in a separate preheated wok or large frying pan, add the spring onions and garlic and stir-fry over a medium-high heat for 1 minute. Add the red peppers and courgettes and stir-fry for 2–3 minutes. Add the coconut milk and curry paste and bring gently to the boil, stirring occasionally. Add the aubergines and chopped coriander, reduce the heat and simmer for 2–3 minutes.

Garnish with sprigs of coriander and serve immediately.

Green Bean & Potato Curry

serves 6

300 ml/10 fl oz vegetable oil

1 tsp white cumin seeds

1 tsp mixed mustard and onion seeds

4 dried red chillies

3 fresh tomatoes, sliced

1 tsp salt

1 tsp finely chopped fresh root ginger

1 tsp crushed fresh garlic

1 tsp chilli powder

200 g/7 oz green beans, diagonally sliced into 2.5-cm/1-inch pieces

2 potatoes, peeled and diced

300 ml/10 fl oz water

chopped fresh coriander and finely sliced green chillies, to garnish

Heat the oil in a large, heavy-based saucepan. Add the white cumin seeds, mustard and onion seeds and dried red chillies, stirring well.

Add the tomatoes to the pan and stir-fry the mixture for 3–5 minutes.

Mix the salt, ginger, garlic and chilli powder together in a bowl and spoon into the saucepan. Blend the whole mixture together.

Add the green beans and potatoes to the saucepan and stir-fry for 5 minutes.

Add the water to the saucepan, reduce the heat and simmer for 10–15 minutes, stirring occasionally. Transfer to a warmed serving dish, garnish with chopped coriander and green chillies and serve.

Okra Curry

serves 4

450 g/1 lb okra

150 ml/5 fl oz vegetable oil

2 onions, sliced

3 fresh green chillies, finely chopped

2 curry leaves

1 tsp salt

1 tomato, sliced

2 tbsp lemon juice

2 tbsp chopped fresh coriander

chapatis, to serve

Rinse the okra and drain thoroughly. Using a sharp knife, chop and discard the ends of the okra. Cut the okra into 2.5-cm/1-inch pieces.

Heat the oil in a large, heavy-based frying pan. Add the onions, green chillies, curry leaves and salt and stir-fry for 5 minutes.

Gradually add the okra, mixing in gently with a slotted spoon, then stir-fry over a medium heat for 12–15 minutes.

Add the sliced tomato to the frying pan and sprinkle over the lemon juice sparingly.

Sprinkle with chopped coriander, cover and leave to simmer for 3–5 minutes. Transfer to serving plates and serve hot with chapatis.

Courgette Curry

serves 4

6 tbsp vegetable oil

1 medium onion, finely chopped

3 fresh green chillies, finely chopped

1 tsp finely chopped fresh root ginger

1 tsp crushed fresh garlic

1 tsp chilli powder

500 g/1 lb 2 oz courgettes, thinly sliced

2 tomatoes, sliced

2 tsp fenugreek seeds

chapatis, to serve

Heat the oil in a large, heavy-based frying pan. Add the onion, green chillies, ginger, garlic and chilli powder to the pan, stirring well to combine.

Add the courgettes and tomatoes to the pan and stir-fry over a medium heat, for 5–7 minutes.

Add the fenugreek seeds to the courgette mixture in the pan and stir-fry over a medium heat for a further 5 minutes, until the vegetables are tender.

Remove the pan from the heat and transfer to serving dishes. Serve hot with chapatis.

Egg & Lentil Curry

serves 4

3 tbsp ghee or vegetable oil

1 large onion, chopped

2 garlic cloves, chopped

2.5 cm/1 inch piece fresh root ginger, chopped

½ tsp minced chilli or chilli powder

1 tsp ground coriander

1 tsp ground cumin

1 tsp paprika

85 g/3 oz split red lentils

450 ml/16 fl oz vegetable stock

225 g/8 oz canned chopped tomatoes

6 eggs

55 ml/2 fl oz coconut milk

2 tomatoes, cut into wedges

salt

sprigs of fresh coriander, to garnish

chapatis, to serve

Heat the ghee in a saucepan, add the onion and cook gently for 3 minutes. Stir in the garlic, ginger, chilli and spices and cook gently, stirring frequently, for 1 minute. Stir in the lentils, stock and tomatoes and bring to the boil. Reduce the heat, cover and simmer, stirring occasionally, for 30 minutes, until the lentils are tender.

Meanwhile, place the eggs in a saucepan of cold water and bring to the boil. Reduce the heat and simmer for 10 minutes. Drain and cover immediately with cold water.

Stir the coconut milk into the lentil mixture and season well with salt. Process the mixture in a blender or food processor until smooth. Return to the pan and heat through.

Shell the hard-boiled eggs and cut into quarters. Divide the hard-boiled egg quarters and tomato wedges between 4 serving plates. Spoon over the hot lentil sauce and garnish with sprigs of coriander. Serve hot with chapatis.

Accompaniments

Onion Bhaji

makes 12

140 g/5 oz besan or gram flour

1 tsp salt

1 tsp ground cumin

1 tsp ground turmeric

1 tsp bicarbonate of soda

½ tsp chilli powder

2 tsp lemon juice

2 tbsp vegetable or groundnut oil, plus extra for deep-frying

2–8 tbsp water

2 onions, thinly sliced

2 tsp coriander seeds, lightly crushed

Sift the besan flour, salt, cumin, turmeric, bicarbonate of soda and chilli powder into a large bowl. Add the lemon juice and the oil, then very gradually stir in just enough water until a batter similar in consistency to single cream forms. Mix in the onions and coriander seeds.

Heat enough oil for deep-frying in a wok, deep-fat fryer or large, heavy-based saucepan until it reaches 180°C/350°F, or until a cube of bread browns in 30 seconds. Without overcrowding the pan, drop in spoonfuls of the onion mixture and fry for 2 minutes, then use tongs to flip the bhajis over and continue frying for a further 2 minutes, or until golden brown.

Immediately remove the bhajis from the oil and drain well on crumpled kitchen paper. Keep the bhajis warm while you continue frying the remaining batter. Serve hot.

Naan Bread

makes 10

900 g/2 lb strong white flour

1 tbsp baking powder

1 tsp sugar

1 tsp salt

300 ml/10 fl oz water, heated to 50°C/122°F

1 egg, beaten

55 g/2 oz ghee, melted, plus extra for rolling out and brushing

Sift the flour, baking powder, sugar and salt into a large mixing bowl and make a well in the centre. Mix together the water and egg, beating until the egg breaks up and is blended with the liquid.

Slowly add the liquid mixture to the dry ingredients, using your fingers to draw in the flour from the sides, until a stiff, heavy dough forms. Shape the dough into a ball and return it to the bowl.

Soak a clean tea towel in hot water, then wring it out and use it to cover the bowl, tucking the ends of the towel under the bowl. Set the bowl aside to let the dough rest for 30 minutes.

Turn out the dough onto a work surface brushed with a little melted ghee and flatten the dough. Gradually sprinkle the dough with the melted ghee and knead to work it in, little by little, until it is completely incorporated. Shape the dough into 10 equal balls.

Resoak the towel in hot water and wring it out again, then place it over the dough balls and leave them to rest and rise for 1 hour.

Meanwhile, put 1 or 2 baking sheets in the oven and preheat the oven to 230°C/450°F/Gas Mark 8 or its highest setting.

Use a lightly greased rolling pin to roll the dough balls into teardrop shapes, about 3 mm/⅛ inch thick. Use crumpled kitchen paper to lightly rub the hot baking sheets with ghee. Arrange the naans on the baking sheets and bake for 5–6 minutes until they are golden brown and lightly puffed. As you take the naans out of the oven, brush with melted ghee and serve immediately.

Vegetarian Samosas

for the filling

1 carrot, diced

200 g/7 oz sweet potato, diced

85 g/3 oz frozen peas

2 tbsp ghee or vegetable oil

1 onion, chopped

1 garlic clove, chopped

2.5-cm/1-inch piece fresh root ginger, grated

1 tsp ground turmeric

1 tsp ground cumin

½ tsp chilli powder

½ tsp garam masala

1 tsp lime juice

salt and pepper

for the pastry

150 g/5½ oz plain flour, plus extra for dusting

3 tbsp butter, diced

4 tbsp warm milk

vegetable oil, for frying

lime wedges, to serve

Bring a saucepan of water to the boil, add the carrot and cook for 4 minutes. Add the sweet potato and cook for 4 minutes, then add the peas and cook for a further 3 minutes. Drain.

Heat the ghee in a saucepan over a medium heat, add the onion, garlic, ginger, spices and lime juice and cook, stirring, for 3 minutes. Add the vegetables and season to taste with salt and pepper. Cook, stirring, for 2 minutes. Remove from the heat and leave to cool for 15 minutes.

To make the pastry, put the flour into a bowl and rub in the butter. Add the milk and mix to form a dough. Knead briefly and divide into 4 pieces. On a lightly floured work surface, roll into balls, then roll out into 17 cm/6½ inches in diameter. Halve each circle, divide the filling between them and brush the edges with water, then fold over into triangles and seal the edges. Heat 2.5 cm/1 inch of oil in a frying pan to 190°C/375°F, or until a cube of bread browns in 30 seconds. Cook the samosas in batches for 3–4 minutes, or until golden. Drain on kitchen paper and serve hot with lime wedges.

Chapatis

makes 6

225 g/8 oz wholemeal flour, sifted, plus extra for dusting

½ tsp salt

150–200 ml/5–7 fl oz water

melted ghee, for brushing

Mix the flour and salt together in a large bowl and make a well in the centre. Gradually stir in enough of the water to make a stiff dough.

Turn out the dough onto a lightly floured surface and knead for 10 minutes, or until it is smooth and elastic. Shape the dough into a ball and place it in the cleaned bowl, then cover with a damp tea towel and leave to rest for 20 minutes.

Divide the dough into 6 equal pieces. Lightly flour your hands and roll each piece of dough into a ball. Meanwhile, heat a large, ungreased, frying pan or griddle over a high heat until very hot and a splash of water 'dances' when it hits the surface.

Working with 1 ball of dough at a time, flatten the dough between your palms, then roll it out on a lightly floured work surface into an 18-cm/7-inch round. Slap the dough onto the hot pan and cook until brown flecks appear on the bottom. Flip the dough over and repeat on the other side.

Flip the dough over again and use a bunched-up tea towel to press down all around the edge. This pushes the steam in the chapati around, causing the chapati to puff up. Continue cooking until the bottom is golden brown, then flip over and repeat this step on the other side.

Brush the chapati with melted ghee and serve, then repeat with the remaining dough balls. Chapatis are best served immediately, as soon as they come out of the pan, but they can be kept warm wrapped in foil for about 20 minutes.

Sag Aloo

serves 4

500 g/1 lb 2 oz fresh spinach leaves

2 tbsp ghee or vegetable oil

1 tsp black mustard seeds

1 onion, halved and sliced

2 tsp garlic and ginger paste

900 g/2 lb waxy potatoes, cut into small chunks

1 tsp chilli powder

125 ml/4 fl oz vegetable stock or water

salt

Bring a large saucepan of water to the boil. Add the spinach leaves and blanch for 4 minutes. Drain well, then tip into a clean tea towel, roll up and squeeze out the excess liquid.

Heat the ghee in a separate saucepan. Add the mustard seeds and cook over a low heat, stirring constantly, for 2 minutes, or until they give off their aroma. Add the onion, and garlic and ginger paste and cook, stirring frequently, for 5 minutes, or until softened.

Add the potatoes, chilli powder and stock and season to taste with salt. Bring to the boil, cover and cook for 10 minutes. Add the spinach and stir it in, then cover and simmer for a further 10 minutes, or until the potatoes are tender. Serve immediately.

Aloo Gobi

serves 4–6

55 g/2 oz ghee or 4 tbsp vegetable or groundnut oil

½ tbsp cumin seeds

1 onion, chopped

4-cm/1½-inch piece fresh root ginger, finely chopped

1 fresh green chilli, deseeded and thinly sliced

450 g/1 lb cauliflower, cut into small florets

450 g/1 lb large waxy potatoes, peeled and cut into large chunks

½ tsp ground coriander

½ tsp garam masala

¼ tsp salt

fresh coriander sprigs, to garnish

Heat the ghee in a flameproof casserole or large frying pan with a tight-fitting lid over a medium-high heat. Add the cumin seeds and stir around for about 30 seconds until they crackle and start to brown.

Immediately stir in the onion, ginger and chilli and stir for 5–8 minutes until the onion is golden.

Stir in the cauliflower and potato, followed by the ground coriander, garam masala and salt, and continue stirring for about 30 seconds longer.

Cover the pan, reduce the heat to the lowest setting and simmer, stirring occasionally, for 20–30 minutes until the vegetables are tender when pierced with the point of a knife. Check occasionally that they aren't sticking to the base of the pan and stir in a little water, if necessary.

Serve garnished with sprigs of coriander.

Matar Paneer

serves 4

85 g/3 oz ghee or 6 tbsp
vegetable or groundnut
oil

350 g/12 oz paneer, cut into
1-cm/½-inch pieces

2 large garlic cloves,
chopped

1-cm/½-inch piece fresh
root ginger, finely
chopped

1 large onion, finely sliced

1 tsp ground turmeric

1 tsp garam masala

¼–½ tsp chilli powder

350 g/12 oz frozen peas or
600 g/1 lb 5 oz fresh peas,
shelled

1 fresh bay leaf

½ tsp salt

125 ml/4 fl oz water

chopped fresh coriander,
to garnish

Heat the ghee in a large frying pan or flameproof casserole with a tight-fitting lid over a medium-high heat. Add as many paneer pieces as will fit in a single layer without overcrowding the pan and cook for about 5 minutes until golden brown on all sides. Use a slotted spoon to remove the paneer and drain on crumpled kitchen paper. Continue, adding a little extra ghee, if necessary, until all the paneer is cooked.

Add the garlic, ginger and onion to the pan and cook, stirring frequently, for 5–8 minutes until the onion is soft, but not brown.

Stir in the turmeric, garam masala and chilli powder and cook for a further 2 minutes.

Add the peas, bay leaf and salt to the pan and stir around. Pour in the water and bring to the boil. Reduce the heat to very low, then cover and simmer for 10 minutes, or until the peas are tender.

Gently return the paneer to the pan. Simmer, stirring gently, until the paneer is heated through. Sprinkle with coriander and serve.

Coconut Rice

serves 4–6

225 g/8 oz basmati rice

450 ml/16 fl oz water

60 g/2¼ oz creamed coconut

2 tbsp mustard oil

1½ tsp salt

toasted flaked coconut, to garnish

Rinse the basmati rice in several changes of water until the water runs clear, then leave to soak for 30 minutes. Drain and set aside until ready to cook.

Bring the water to the boil in a small saucepan, stir in the creamed coconut until it dissolves and then set aside.

Heat the mustard oil in a large frying pan or saucepan with a lid over a high heat until it smokes. Turn off the heat and leave the mustard oil to cool completely.

When you are ready to cook, reheat the mustard oil over a medium-high heat. Add the rice and stir until all the grains are coated in oil. Add the water with the dissolved coconut and bring to the boil.

Reduce the heat to as low as possible, stir in the salt and cover the pan tightly. Simmer, without lifting the lid, for 8–10 minutes until the grains are tender and all the liquid is absorbed.

Turn off the heat and use 2 forks to mix the rice. Re-cover the pan and leave the rice to stand for 5 minutes. Serve garnished with toasted flaked coconut.

Fruit & Nut Pilau

serves 4–6

225 g/8 oz basmati rice

450 ml/16 fl oz water

½ tsp saffron threads

1 tsp salt

25 g/1 oz ghee or 2 tbsp vegetable or groundnut oil

55 g/2 oz blanched almonds

1 onion, thinly sliced

1 cinnamon stick, broken in half

seeds from 4 green cardamom pods

1 tsp cumin seeds

1 tsp black peppercorns, lightly crushed

2 bay leaves

3 tbsp finely chopped dried mango

3 tbsp finely chopped dried apricots

2 tbsp sultanas

55 g/2 oz pistachio nuts, chopped

Rinse the basmati rice in several changes of water until the water runs clear, then leave to soak for 30 minutes. Drain and set aside until ready to cook.

Boil the water in a small saucepan. Add the saffron threads and salt, remove from the heat and set aside to infuse.

Heat the ghee in a large saucepan with a tight-fitting lid over a medium-high heat. Add the almonds and stir them around until golden brown, then immediately use a slotted spoon to scoop them out of the pan.

Add the onion to the pan and cook, stirring frequently, for 5–8 minutes until golden, but not brown. Add the spices and bay leaves to the pan and stir them around for about 30 seconds.

Add the rice to the pan and stir until the grains are coated with ghee. Add the saffron-infused water and bring to the boil. Reduce the heat to as low as possible, stir in the dried fruit and cover the pan tightly. Simmer, without lifting the lid, for 8–10 minutes until the grains are tender and all the liquid is absorbed.

Turn off the heat and use 2 forks to mix the almonds and pistachios into the rice. Re-cover the pan and leave to stand for 5 minutes before serving.

Spiced Basmati Pilau

serves 4

500 g/1 lb 2 oz basmati rice

175 g/6 oz broccoli, trimmed

6 tbsp vegetable oil

2 large onions, chopped

225 g/8 oz mushrooms, sliced

2 garlic cloves, crushed

6 cardamom pods, split

6 whole cloves

8 black peppercorns

1 cinnamon stick or piece of cassia bark

1 tsp ground turmeric

1.2 litres/2 pints vegetable stock or water

55 g/2 oz seedless raisins

55 g/2 oz unsalted pistachios, coarsely chopped

salt and pepper

Place the rice in a sieve and wash well under cold running water. Drain. Trim off most of the broccoli stalk and cut the head into small florets, then quarter the stalk lengthways and cut diagonally into 1-cm/½-inch pieces.

Heat the oil in a large saucepan. Add the onions and broccoli stalks and cook over a low heat, stirring frequently, for 3 minutes. Add the mushrooms, rice, garlic and spices and cook for 1 minute, stirring, until the rice is coated in oil.

Add the stock and season to taste with salt and pepper. Stir in the broccoli florets and return the mixture to the boil. Cover, reduce the heat and cook over a low heat for 15 minutes without uncovering the pan.

Remove the pan from the heat and leave the pilau to stand for 5 minutes without uncovering. Remove the whole spices, add the raisins and pistachios and gently fork through to fluff up the grains. Serve the pilau hot.

Lemon Rice

serves 4–6

225 g/8 oz basmati rice

25 g/1 oz ghee or 2 tbsp vegetable or groundnut oil

1 tsp nigella seeds

450 ml/16 fl oz water

finely grated rind and juice of 1 large lemon

1½ tsp salt

¼ tsp ground turmeric

Rinse the basmati rice in several changes of water until the water runs clear, then leave to soak for 30 minutes. Drain and set aside until ready to cook.

Heat the ghee in a large saucepan with a tight-fitting lid over a medium-high heat. Add the nigella seeds and rice and stir until all the grains are coated in ghee. Add the water and bring to the boil.

Reduce the heat to as low as possible, stir in half the lemon juice, the salt and turmeric and cover the pan tightly. Simmer, without lifting the lid, for 8–10 minutes until the grains are tender and all the liquid is absorbed.

Turn off the heat and use 2 forks to mix the lemon rind and remaining juice into the rice. Re-cover the casserole and leave the rice to stand for 5 minutes before serving.

Plantain Chips

serves 4

4 ripe plantains

1 tsp mild, medium or hot
curry powder, to taste

vegetable or groundnut oil,
for deep-frying

mango chutney, to serve

Peel the plantains, then cut crossways into 3-mm/$1/8$-inch slices. Put the slices in a bowl, sprinkle over the curry powder and use your hands to lightly toss together.

Heat enough oil for deep-frying in a wok, deep-fat fryer or large heavy-based saucepan to 180°C/350°F, or until a cube of bread browns in 30 seconds. Add as many plantain slices as will fit in the pan without overcrowding and fry for 2 minutes, or until golden.

Remove the plantain chips from the pan with a slotted spoon and drain well on crumpled kitchen paper. Serve hot with mango chutney.

Coconut Sambal

makes about 140 g/5 oz

½ fresh coconut or
125 g/4½ oz desiccated
coconut

2 fresh green chillies,
deseeded or not, to taste,
and chopped

2.5-cm/1-inch piece fresh
root ginger, peeled and
finely chopped

4 tbsp chopped fresh
coriander

2 tbsp lemon juice,
or to taste

2 shallots, very finely
chopped

If you are using a whole coconut, use a hammer and nail to punch a hole in the 'eye' of the coconut, then pour out the water from the inside and reserve. Use the hammer to break the coconut in half, then peel half and chop.

Put the coconut and chillies in a food processor and process for about 30 seconds until finely chopped. Add the ginger, coriander and lemon juice and process again.

If the mixture seems too dry, stir in about 1 tablespoon of coconut water or water. Stir in the shallots and serve immediately, or cover and chill until required. This will keep its fresh flavour in the refrigerator for up to 3 days.

Mango Chutney

makes about 250 g/9 oz

1 large mango, about 400 g/14 oz, peeled, stoned and finely chopped

2 tbsp lime juice

1 tbsp vegetable or groundnut oil

2 shallots, finely chopped

1 garlic clove, finely chopped

2 fresh green chillies, deseeded and finely sliced

1 tsp black mustard seeds

1 tsp coriander seeds

5 tbsp grated jaggery or light brown sugar

5 tbsp white wine vinegar

1 tsp salt

pinch of ground ginger

Put the mango in a non-metallic bowl with the lime juice and set aside.

Heat the oil in a large frying pan or saucepan over a medium-high heat. Add the shallots and cook for 3 minutes. Add the garlic and chillies and stir for a further 2 minutes, or until the shallots are soft, but not brown. Add the mustard and coriander seeds and then stir around.

Add the mango to the pan with the jaggery, vinegar, salt and ground ginger and stir around. Reduce the heat to its lowest setting and simmer for 10 minutes until the liquid thickens and the mango becomes sticky.

Remove from the heat and leave to cool completely. Transfer to an airtight container, cover and chill for 3 days before using. Store in the refrigerator and use within 1 week.

Raita

serves 4–6

1 large piece of cucumber, about 300 g/10½ oz, rinsed

1 tsp salt

400 ml/14 fl oz natural yogurt

½ tsp sugar

pinch of ground cumin

2 tbsp chopped fresh coriander or mint

chilli powder, to garnish

Lay a clean tea towel flat on the work surface. Coarsely grate the unpeeled cucumber directly onto the towel. Sprinkle with ½ teaspoon of the salt, then gather up the towel and squeeze until all the excess moisture is removed from the cucumber.

Put the yogurt into a bowl and beat in the remaining ½ teaspoon of salt, along with the sugar and cumin. Stir in the grated cucumber. Taste and add extra salt, if you like. Cover and chill until ready to serve.

Stir in the chopped coriander and transfer to a serving bowl. Sprinkle with chilli powder and serve.

Lime Pickle

makes about 225 g/8 oz

12 limes, halved and deseeded

115 g/4 oz salt

70 g/2½ oz chilli powder

25 g/1 oz mustard powder

25 g/1 oz ground fenugreek

1 tbsp ground turmeric

300 ml/10 fl oz mustard oil

15 g/½ oz yellow mustard seeds, crushed

½ tsp asafoetida

Cut each lime half into 4 pieces and pack them into a large sterilised jar, sprinkling over the salt at the same time. Cover and leave to stand in a warm place for 10–14 days, or until the limes have turned brown and softened.

Mix the chilli powder, mustard powder, fenugreek and turmeric together in a small bowl and add to the jar of limes. Stir to mix, then re-cover and leave to stand for 2 days.

Transfer the lime mixture to a heatproof bowl. Heat the mustard oil in a heavy-based frying pan.

Add the mustard seeds and asafoetida to the pan and cook, stirring constantly, until the oil is very hot and just beginning to smoke. Pour the oil and spices over the limes and mix well. Cover and leave to cool. When cool, pack into a sterilised jar, seal and store in a sunny place for 1 week before serving.

Chilli & Onion Chutney

makes about 225 g/8 oz

1–2 fresh green chillies, deseeded or not, to taste, and finely chopped

1 small fresh bird's eye chilli, deseeded or not, to taste, and finely chopped

1 tbsp white wine vinegar or cider vinegar

2 onions, finely chopped

2 tbsp fresh lemon juice

1 tbsp sugar

3 tbsp chopped fresh coriander, mint or parsley, or a combination of herbs

salt

chilli flower, to garnish

To make the chilli flower garnish, use a sharp knife to make four cuts lengthways along the chilli. Place the point of the knife about 1 cm/ ½ inch from the stem end and cut towards the tip. Put the chilli in a bowl of iced water and let stand for 25–30 minutes, or until the cut edges have spread out to form a flower shape.

Put the chillies in a small non-metallic bowl with the vinegar, stir around and then drain. Return the chillies to the bowl and stir in the onions, lemon juice, sugar and herbs, then add salt to taste.

Leave to stand at room temperature or cover and chill for 15 minutes. Garnish with the chilli flower before serving.